WAY TOO WEST

Julien Poirier

Bootstrap Press
2015

First Edition

ISBN 13: 978-0-9886108-4-2

In 2013 the whole poem appeared in installments on Filip Marinovich's blog, "Wolfman Librarian." Nick Whittington published the opening slice of "Book 12" in his superb journal *Amerarcana* in 2014. And I will never forget John Sakkis for recording the poem's baby steps in his magazine *Both Both* in 2012. —Julien

Typesetting & book design by Derek Fenner.
Cover art & design by Jake Hout.
Text edited by Nathaniel Farrell.
Songs notated by Justin Dudley.

Bootstrap Press books are designed and edited by Derek Fenner and Ryan Gallagher.

West Coast:
365 Euclid Ave #107
Oakland, CA 94610

East Coast:
31 Wyman Street
Lowell, MA 01852

www.bootstrappress.org

For the losers

On all the old roads she goes ahead
For her Troupe a dash of friction
is ever the solution
to a pang or a pitfall.
Many Miracles
so-called, are merely so:
Resource
at wit's end,
a terse joiner of epics.

These magicians and natural acrobats
lavished practice with a oneness
of faction on the crowd that paid up
to a quarter to see them
cheat certain
death, physique and spar alloyed
to principled interdependence, an allegiance
to drift ensconced in sleight of hand,
selves averaged by the wilderness of others.

They liked to stop
in underrated lands
with no language, yet
where language languished, numb from use
or loafed, laughingly, its youth
in flashing ringlets
of authority.
The air there was sweet
to the irredeemable seeker.

The constant earth shrinks from words
and laps its sun,
its bitter tides
even out. Tropics commute...

They were all rolling in goose pimples,
bolting with cocky gambol
and faulty hunches
conscripted to honey-tongued quagmire.
The rare brick of doubt.

Procrastinators,
        dispensers of omens, jugglers,
               white liar loners,
self-flagellating egoists,
        teenage hypnotists,
               enthusiasts of cults they don't belong to,
solstice addicts,
        piano tuners,
           hitch-hiking urban farmers, prototypes,
zoo deniers,
        banshees, horseshit gazers,
             shoestring theorists,
trumpet abusers...

But maybe a certain future
        historian, making fast friends
            with routs
in courting ramblers
        who flickered when they breezed
between two skids
        of popular cargo
           and the sliding doors of the Farralones
would say she heard
        wild hayseeds tramping inland
           canyons buzzed,
Scarcity's rites
        decoyed on candy rings—
           with their guttersnipes
and baby pitbulls
        swaddled in filthy Pendletons...

Glinka the Sailor, born Glinka the Tub

                                   came up in Visalia, found

a single white sateen Sunday glove

                                 on the tentative bridge

the streetcar geode

                strung out

                        to episodic waves, her pinkynail

closely matched

                crabs on the meteor

                         the Pacific Coast Highway

warm like a thick plate

                  flipped from the washer

                            in back of the diner

she picked mint

                for tea, manganese in the saddle

                               of Planned Parenthood

waiting room magazine,

                      candy cane street lamps

in January

              hometeam in the cellar.

                        Hot nights you could smell

the black Sicilian grapes,

                  union-made tubes

                           in the stained cherry radio

on lay away

14

Kyoto Showboat
                was said to be touched
                                or maybe
psychic
        when he found the satellite
                          in the Western Jungle
It had plowed a littoral
                green room in the undergrowth
and mangled scuba gear
                poured from its mouth.
This reticent Samurai
            like a gardener at dawn
                            pissed on the wires
that were singeing the fronds

————

That was the night of the big dance in the underground,
they were blasting the tunnel
                rounded with radium
                        in honor of exiles
braided ramps
        framed by shells
the Liberty Globe
        in its mud-packed sextant
—The sleepless old people
        clutching at nightgowns
and things that seemed precious
        when it was almost too late
—The coal train that shook them
        down Christmas rails

        punched out a saloon door
        swizzled the piano stool
        ran off the sewer grate
            past a waterfall
and row of off-duty cabs

Then through the tall white pillars, flood-limed, many feet up.
Apprehension, even terror among the passengers...

Greinke and Earl
                    once trafficked in carpets
                                        for Lambik a lady
in Redding,
                    but they didn't know Lambik
                                        was really a poet
and the carpets they finnangled
                            the missing poets.
The Byzantine whirl
                    of her duplicity
                                    flocked the marbles
in the Capitol of Nectar
                            and its ashen torture chambers, sparkled
in lyric salons
                    esteemed by the occupying force

        Look upon these two chastened spaniels
        and wonder that they'd one day change
        the face of slapstick.

"O! what a beautiful flami-- pigeon."

                              Fending tenderfeet
        Radical and Blasphemous
                                        Deciduous blasters
                    splatter vinyl
hobnail
            bubble gum cigarette
                                hardpan cardinal door
                                            room wind
                        surfer early
bird disco
            fries traffic
                    cones on the Southern
                                    Cone the grape
soap flake why the
                long face a snap of old
Olema it's too
                early for My Sharona De
                                Do Ron Ron glitch
crackling into young
                Lundy's
                        breakfast counter starched
whippet peak onion dis-
                    mantled on the nacreous
                                skillet crackling
plastic speech bubble rose in the rose rows the

                    cheek to fake sleep

```
* * * * *      * * * * * *    * *
*     THE YARROWS
*     Most Accident-Prone Family      *
*          in the World               *
* * * * * * * * * * * *    * * *
```

Cousin Lucy and her beau came, baked the cake
And of course Uncle Dilan brought along a free jazz quintet of mates
Late for a gig in the City.
Didn't he meet Amber there, cuffed by local flowers as she'd later appear
In the entry hall of the Yarrow Pile
With a young, sly Dilan in the frame?
Of course, yeah, he met her through
Day, who married them,
Art and Eloise I mean.
Art's radical journalist friend from the LNS, the one who spilled the beans
On ConEd in New York. I can't believe you remember that
But sure, he was ordained by mail, started a sound
Studio in San Luis Obispo
Circa disco. But most of the Yarrows stayed put in L.A.
No doubt, had they been invited
They put would have stayed.

The elopement, the tryst with est—
Was that before Amber's breakdown
After Dilan broke his leg?
How did it happen
Anyway, I never got the story.
By stepping into a bucket from repairing
A molding in the entry
Hall of the Pile—it was rather gory
And ironic in light of his horse's name,
"Hole in the Bucket." I do remember that part—

        "Hole in the Bucket closing fast!"

It always came to me when I'd pass
Another car.

So there you are, Dilan
Laid up in the Pile with a double fracture when Amber vanishes
The day Eloise flies to India and
Oh, don't tell me
That's when Art was betrayed by Cyprus
When Cyprus—took the negatives

And sold them twice over.
And Art arrives in Heathrow
From Bombay—and on his way
To meet
Carlotta at the hotel is arrested.

When did Art learn she'd run away?
Well, it was five days
Before he could reach
Eloise who informed him
Of the freeze on their accounts:
His best friend and partner
Whom he'd mentored,
Loved
Had cleaned him out
And run off with his blind adopted daughter...

Chico   Mariposa   San Rafael

Eureka

                    Hole in the Bucket closing fast

Lakeport   Redding   Los
                                                              Gatos

            Hat Creek
                    Hole in the Bucket closing fast

                                                   Fort

BRAGG

m   e   n   d   o   c   i   n   o

                    Enci   no

Nevada City

                    Hole in the Bucket closing fast

                                        Fruitvale   Pasa

dena   Dublin   ECHO PARK

Hole in the Bucket closing fast

Here's one of Jed—in his Eagle Scout scrubs
His cheek this side of glum, a scullion in those epaulets
Magpie eyelet pins and sashes
The bunting of his nonchalance,
Squinting into the sun
Days after the 4th
Of July accident with the hat—Ah
Art's! No, Jed

Sr's. Right
Right—his
Grandpa's peaked cap from the War,
Tipped back in a New Delhi bunker with a nothing hand, gin
Tonic with British officers he abhorred.
That hat never saw combat, but with a Jumbo Ground Bloom
Flower Jed singed the laurels on its bill
And cried behind the hothouse—Carlotta's
Folly: There, just over the hill
—He was twelve in 1984,
A gifted squinter
Apprenticed by stepping stone to the Yarrow

"Pile" as everyone had it: a tramp Italianate with a few stories
Up from holly on the fault, sage brush,
Palomino bulrush footnote sown
By a Chinese freighter (or maybe a Moroccan corsair) its balcony
Sweep of the Pacific clipped by blue
Trash incinerator, the sound wall reticulated
To bitmap air brakes from exclusive subdivisions
Soared the roar—by pneumatic rube—stegosaurs in gel caps
To pillows on the top floor
Of the Pile which Sally, Jed's little sister
At 17
An excellent student with no truck in school
Held alone—not counting
Three confidantes and partisans who would "sneak"
In late at night (the Pile's door always unlocked
Or ajar to the fog) to stage,
Though only three were sure,
An ambush of the Patriarchy "whether
They draw or not" through novel
Poetry, arriving (strict Yarrow

Luck) minutes into the fire sale on Patriarchy

On the quad: Two bursts on a horn at the drive-in, then once more
At the riots on Sproul where Eloise (a "co-ed")
Got teargassed and Art was still, but just, pledged to the singing frat
And Vietnam ("I thought we had to close the door")
An unlikely kiss
Hinging on a wrist watch, in fact they stood
Right in the shadow of my head—right where Jed
Stood, moving the tip of his Red Army
Knife through paint flakes just below
The kitchen window
Frame—rotten planks—the flake
Parasailing in fully juiced hothouse
Bulbs—stood twinned
While a good friend radical journalist for the LNS flubbed the cloth (alterego'd
A sound studio in uhm
San Leandro during Carter), everyone garlanded by local flowers,
A free jazz quartet of mates
Late for a gig in the city laid it down on stage (plywood
Trompe l'oeil parade crepe, cryogenic in the basement)
—And Cousin Lucy baked the cake ... Jed already growing
In Eloise—Where was I
Conceived?

(Yarrow, a.k.a.)

Old Mans Pepper

Nose Bleed

Carpenters Weed

Bloodwort

Devils Nettle

Bad Mans Plaything

Before the
          native grasses were
                    grazed to
                    death +
                    droughtd
out, CA grasslands
wld hv been green
smoke not gold
                    "blue-eyed" grass w/
yellow petals and sword

grass you'd find sleeping sleeping in
Coastal Prairies above cliffs
along the landlocked back-
track of sandy beaches—
perennial grasses
                    plated by

wind...
          clay under
                    (sandboxes)

the sand its heat + poor minerals

          SALT RUSH
          JUKEBOX

in SF marshes—
cheap flip for dirty energy
Airports, Golden Gate
Fields where Epoxy dunked

                    Hole in the Bucket for
                              keeps
                              and
                              Dilan
                              too
                              and
                              all
                              Yarrows
                                   ever

Tract homes, crop marks
          Dumps...

Telegraph Weed

        (a dishglove flower) and

      Tidytips,
   a bouquet of

         for Eloise
           and "Indian Pinks"

sprouting from leaky
      drinking fountains

            <u>Red Huckleberry</u>

up Scow Canyon eliding electric
fences like the milky tips of drum sticks
rolled off
        iceberg loaves of lettuce
in a waxed hailstone Lotto
crate abandoned on Beckett
            alley, China-
town—telephone wires clear up
to Mendocino
       County line, at the Pile—coiled
ditchweed

      Red Fes
         cue
            to the
              Fed's res
                 cue

      Germander Speedwell
      <u>YOU KNOW IT</u>
      climbing off his private

jet, slovenly baggy (in a ringer for my green
Jed Sr. raincoat)—"Limey"—
brandishes that morning's *News of the
World* w/ color snapshot of YOU above the
fold for fotographers to re-
frame—slapping 2 fingers onto
pic: "Feast your eyes on the best band
on earth, you slobs!" Then: "Stozzer!"
(which means "Fuck off" in dream German)

"no brain at all,
simply no brain at
all"—Nelson Algren
(on a "softclothes
dick" in Chi)(critic
or censor) lit a Balkan

Sobranie (wild guess) in that self-
same church
         stoop where fleer decades
later Carlotta waltzed a red checked
table cloth to bluff the hummingbird
down from the rafters—and on the
soup kitchen doorstep, a sliced Bosc

viola

     ~ in Red Hook, NY ~

        at sunrise
     Grizzly Peak by dusk

...rolling up Masonic in the canceled cop
car w/ the battering ram fresh bolted wld
ruther be buttering rum in her crushable
sun hat blowzy rose sunglasses freckled
pistons rooted to steerage
     —How you gonna square that with her
being blind? See

     the frog jeweler
     finishing flashing
his counterfeit 5000 euro

        note
            on the
        Gloucester canal
            in a soap bubble study

"and live like a pig
    in the clover
        inside of huge Mtns of snow"—

        For the original is essentially as mad
as the imitator,
            early one warm twilight,
Carlotta's underused vibrator in the drawer
—But then again
maybe a vibrator gets better with age, like Mickey's Big Mouths
—While the blowhard she ran off with, my
"Uncle"
                        Cyprus—Ha! is just warming

up...

            "U.S. lack of social *cohe*
            sion inspires far-out a
            ssertion of tribal *identities*
            in popular culture GLAM
            PFLANZE Jelly Roll Mor
            ton's diamond eye-tooth SMALL
            TALK FIGHT
            There are no more private hells.
            If there ever was.
                        were."
                        —And she has only
to sit there?
to win the argument

        ...must find an equal otherworld...

DOWN & OUT CATALYSTS

Walking across campus dead leaves crunching under our feet I turn
to Professor Fancygirlhouse—
                                        "I love the start of winter, I'm falling in love
with this girl, I can't help thinking of her
eyes when I see those
crows—ducks?
                        on the empty branches.
The thought that I might wind up
next to her in bed tonite makes me dizzy, my
God I love New England and turkey leftovers hot apple cider mulled
wine and mirthless fairy lights in the Greyhound
vestibule."
"Your joy is fertilized by insane wars,"
says Professor Fancygirlhouse.
                                "Yes," I
say. "All I can do about it is stand here scratching
paint flakes off the family house with my Chairman
Mao butterknife, so off-the-wall *equal* it proves joy
has no need of those fertilizers."
                                "To thrill us,
to honor all those living
through this fevered dance,"
says Prof. F.
                        "Reality is perfect," I say,
"and nothing could be other than.
Including our need to struggle."
                                "People are not
as similar as they look,"
sz Prof. Fancygirlhouse, swiping open the lab door.
"Some believe in the perfectibility of Authority
—and they live that belief;

"But all people are fundamentally incompetent managers of each other."

.   .   .   .

Judy Collins and David Mamet get coffee at the diner Sunday eve NYC.
Mamet, perhaps in love with her, once more expresses his disgust with
the Muppet Show—in general, but especially with her turn as a guest star.
His clashing emotions crest in a morbid funk. Taxis slide past the tall
window, neon bullet shells, clouds racing for the pink slip. The L.A.
River, like a heavily sedated Kong, snaps open its eyes—Midnight and the
River is incapable of reaching out to take Judy Collins in its arms,
incipient scars of a bad speed habit *projected* on her face. (What era the
cabs? 80s?) Soon she will return to her modest Gramercy flat decorated
with exquisite Oceanic art,

       CLICKING HER ELECTRONIC CIGARETTE
       in the Lite-Brite arroyo,
                      her coyote mint fan

       rippling granite static
       on vast Sierran screens

and he still hasn't told her ... *he still hasn't spoken his heart.*

It's obvious for instance that "terror" is what we call "loss of control." Fear of terror
happening is fear of losing control. "Anxiety" is what we call awareness that we're not
in control. The thing I'm most afraid of tonight is dying because by dying I would put my
family in danger. I can't "know" that they'll be "OK" unless I'm here to make it OK by
controlling the ongoing emergencies that define this terror-filled world.

OK?

"All right, Lester, go ahead and
put those holes in those trees before
Mother Nature gets here."
                    —Woody Woodpecker

Dinner with a surprise guest:

  William F. Buckley Jr.

who tries to see down Doozy's dress
while cooing like a baby—
                    His date's my college study
buddy, Jenny Nguen
Dr.
Deadpan, dressed to kill.
Makes a good foil to the famous grin, like
but just like, if I may
countermand your edict of yesterday
        and go there, Flat Stanley
made
to his kickstand, the Swami from Pinole.
Flat Stanley. Oh
rack your brains, *You*
know: that nasty macaw.
How the Swami played a Latino Bogart to the pink bird.
What was the name of that actor
kid
superfine, Jenny broke his heart at Christmastime

                We 3 Kings of Orient are
                In the market for a used car

They descend, and now must rise, in a black stretch
Hummer—Mom
smells him on the smoky wind, cocks up her iron
Heh!—dashes in sockfeet
                to damn his eyes: Buckley jumps.
Then it's on

to the theater, ZB on the service stairs
takes a slug of half-froze plonk:

        "Swan won't be found sitting in front of Adobe anymore
        on his hill of beans"

And I'm squirming in my leopard spots.
Something's gone wrong.
None of the poets will talk to me.
I keep going back to Doozy's apt. but she's never there,
all I see is a flash of teeth, too much lipstick.
The poet Mike McClure is chasing her
on his treesap motorbike.
I hear his voice* breaking on her answering machine
as I "break in." 3rd or 4th time
in, I realize her apt. is one of a string
of apts getting more littered and pissed up by the night.
Her apt. is up there on the 60s apt. balcony catwalk
and everytime I go back it's more ruined, dying and falling to pieces,
though I note her bed's been slept in
each time, sheets twisted different—
Maybe her and Mike...
Where's his motorbike?
—And on the wall
superheated fast clouds of ants swirl, collide
stream out over the cracked paint,
like sparrows in the sunset over Fez medina.

> * "Darting through the darkness
> with our smiles for boots"

Doozy in the one-piece parachute
jumpsuit w/ epaulets + curls sprung
o'er smeary lashes + scruff blazed on bedhead
            Louche in her nook, black coffee
in boardwalk mug,
Jed
bandy like a waterskier
in boxers w/ the indigo seahorses
dials tomato
        breaks yolks
with bamboo spatula
& pickled jalapeño from a cold jar, chants
obsequiously silent
grace, slides the plate over webbed corner of the Sun-
day Planta Nova Now with which she is taken
w/ a capsule review of *Dangerous Liaisons*
w/ clip n save coupons for places w/in a block
w/ the teaser

> "To be shut in by the closed eyes
> of someone who doesn't think you exist"

w/ the classifieds:

    contiguous   Plebiscite

                  phlybicis

wzino

w/ Human turds in Clorox halos / galloped yesterday from a breached Hercules refinery
w/ Astro-logical Trade Routes "silver like rope on the fingertips of your eyes"

and

w/ C. Bengston, parking lot attendant, who swims under the bridge looking for girls...

"Amazing to think these waters once ran so thick w/ pink salmon you cld walk on yr hands
cross the delta on their exuberant bumpers.
                        [strips a fold]
Listen to this:

32

*"Going down the highway
looking for an ordinary motivation,
following your song
from station to station"*
—Gail Southern

        down the highway
to Escondido
      "infra-neural"
outside that same bodega
we would dig the cognoscenti
reform again when it gets cold—
Floorlength scarf flung feathered
        low lights in the theater,
          "Vanumanutagi"
held over
   "Quien Sabe"
at the Syndrome:
Shrine of the spray plastic house set,
even the hectic
house made it a sleeper
      hit,
         summer showers
in the palms
hanging threads of pure wook.
        Fingerpainted line-up
on the curb in front of Candler's
sporting really self-consciously
normal haircuts,
deepsixing wet bandanas and Maalox
      —Accurate Comix of History
pink
    popcorn bricks
Voodoo bells
Ancient babies on the old st.
like gondoliers mummified in cocoa beans
      drifting through
a reconnaissance of hearses—
Frost it in shred works:
        Camo Cake
an Abrams
     Sandcake
for a newborn democracy
as green in the eye as
the cat at the Yemenie-American
      Grocers Assn.

"following your song
from station to station"

Cañon

Can yawn

Due west

Duet

with the wily San Lorenzo
one
           torches in rapids the exurbs
of sudden money,
                    reciting "A Blue Grass Penelope"
down broad aves
lined with Clippers
bans

SEASON TICKETS ON SALE ANARCH 9

escape brain flashes—

           Flibbertigibbet
           Crane stalks the manmade
           Lick

                    —monocles the night clouds
through skull's oven
broadcasts the charged,
backwards wind

"All forms of human infatuation"—Baudelaire

           to the hole in the Milky Head

sing, Doozy, sing!

           Galactic Black
           Dressed in black
           Dress slacks

crouched at Gunshot Point, shooting iron a mottled rainbow

           Chipt her tooth
           On a slice of Ironkids
           White

trout,   *took aim*

> Gift-wrecked—
> Revering gold's
> Transvagrancy

—while munching on Cheetos / like the cocoon of the Blue Morpho

> Blake Bart

walking double of spilled blood.

/

"Shrewd," says Doozy, bunching the Arts Page. "Say that like Johnny Cash Robot: 'Thanks for the braille on the wine bottle.'"

"Fiscally drunken derivatives traders," says Jed in the voice of the Johnny Cash Robot.

"Here actress Doozy Eaton and her coterie of talented friends..."

Went into outer space, but all you did was sit around reading magazines. So I beat you up. You fell into a *witchy boite* and danced the night away. It was all pretend: Religious pretend, like *A Place in the Sun*. No sound. Bouquets of flowers from every planet. Or a series of grainy photos of a passenger jet plunging toward the ocean

> or "the shore of water

> "She's granulated"

- - - - - - - - - - - - - -

BY PERMISSION AND UNDER THE IMMEDIATE PATRONAGE
OF THE
PLANTA NOVA PSYCHIC
~ and latterday ELKS CLUB ~ INSTITUTE

ON FRIDAY, OCTOBER 13, A DAY
OF Renegade Art and Rampant Publick Fucking
FOR THE BENEFIT OF MRS.
CIJA BELLIS née APHRA BEHN

THE GOLDEN STATE'S CELEBRATED
? GOALIES OF ELDRITCH ?
☆ PREVIOUS TO THEIR DEPARTURE FOR "THE WESTERN JUNGLE" ☆

FOR THE FIRST TIME!
Ms. B. will present UNDERLINED PORTRAITS of Herself in sundry Characters.

Aphra Behn -- Poetess and double agent for CROWNED ANARCHY

"C.B.B." -- Her estranged brother blinded while defending God and country.

* Ms. B. will read palms for train fare *
* She blows up a balloon with her eye! *

.... The evening will commence with the ZERO GRAVITY SLAPSTICK....
of GREINKE and [TELL IT LIKE IT IS] EARL

"THE CAT'S CRA-RAVELSTE IN DLE KID"

NEW ST. ARLIGHT furniture

★ The Renowned Troupe...!
★ NO ONE TURNED AWAY FOR LACK OF $

THE CAT'S CRADLE KID

Jagadis Ravelstein
                        invented a card game
to play in the rain
                —with Cija Bellis
                                heiress of exterminators
her fiddle a termite
                Ark: wood (she cut) half
                                        watermelon / he streamed
even in air-conditioned aisles
                        stealing charity chocolate
                bars, baby
                        aspirin—redwood saplings
were hyper-attentive
                to his tread.

A filthy elf with sideburns,
the Cat's Cradle Kid

and his allies...

You're acquainted with Jagadis, the Cat's Cradle Kid
Who wore dates on his feet
The pits, such weird
Books—and books he read at cost
To glitzy Kress, like *Jane Eyre*
He dressed with a casual psychotropic air
In a lettuce leaf, or *Vineland*
Coming out, dressed by the Kid's eyes,
A how-to crib sheet for Elven spies—

Or how he caught a ride in a turquoise pebble
Paratransit van
With gold braid bangle sleeper blinds
From San Rafael to Venice in a shot
The ex-D.A. of Berkeley (Christ!
But would the D.A. lie?) behind the wheel

And his Irish girlfriend
Gifting Jag a painful boner—telekinetic
Her knotted bag of candied ginger
Till he whacked off at the self-made artichoke
Moonlit Gilroy Union Hall
Rest stop stall
Like to Sally Yarrow later
Sprinted through the mister ("The hiss of the mister
That was ace!") with a bottle of whiskey
In one fist
And a fistful of the wrong stolen letters:
The hero of a mocumentary
In sync with his blood sister
Stashed black paper in the wall panel, presto!
As if wiping rain from a mirror—
There appears on the scene a biker
More grouchy than menacing,
Infatuated with a genetic overthrow—
Cob bombs at Monsanto—their nightly unfolding
Ghost story where Jagadis dies shaving
On a Burbank cigar shop stoop shut for Christmas
Uh, looks like a wedge of pie on the Italian
Riviera, hedge like a halved plastic
Security clip on the Fall line
T-shirt—rusty wire banding
CA plates to his sparkly green bike

Coming up on Fink Rd

milky plastic like snot wiped on the road cuts

Um

Croak Rd to Anderson

("Means Split Pea")

and the fake Mission bells of Hotel de Oro,

working for gravity

WORKING FOR GRAVITY
by Jed Yarrow

TRANSYLVANIA, DECEMBER 27, 2038—These days, Jagadis Ravelstein works it all out at his pied a terre in this booming tropical megalopolis. He has the crushed-petal eyelids of an offputtingly precocious kid but is now a shrunk man, quite bald, whose intensity when he focuses on anything is so intense that he looks completely bored.

His art for many years has followed this pattern:

(FROM THE CATALOGUE OF HIS ONE-MAN SHOW "GOALIES OF ELDRITCH" LISBON 1997)

er, and never more than one found
stone per sculpture, they may be what
70s "organic" architecture* aspired to
be, albeit in miniature, very large
rough-but-smooth-bored river rocks
shot with curvaceous orifices, they
have the presence of stone-age hand
axes displaced by the meticulous
affect of an intensely private mast
er. Some acquaintances at the show
seemed surprised I like them so
much considering what goes on
between him and Sally—I mean
they seem to think I should be
disgusted that Jagadis is boinking
my sister or by the manner in which
they imagine he's boinking her. Well
fuck them. Why am I raving? is it
the night? the company of the sexy
waitress who held my hand all the
way up past the Praça da Figueira
through the church graveyard (which
we'll have to re-cross on the way
back down to meet Mom and Dad
stranded on the cafe patio) and who's
still clutching the light green gummed
pad on which she'd begun taking
our orders?—Or am I getting drunk
on the open-air (though minute,
beamed) gallery on the hilltop, all
given over to Jag's work—drunk
on the first-drink lighting. And
behind the bar there's a Ravelstein
esque lamp: angel food plastic,
those signature orifices. I was taken

with it upon our arrival, the first
"piece" I saw, and now wonder
if it's cheap
        and if so, is the whole
set-up cheap? did Jagadis
sell out? license out
his look
to make a killing?
I decide I like it anyway.

Fast fortune in tar and feathers.

* modular eggshell polymer igloo commode habitation binocular westward orientation

Blue Lake #6
(sold)
                Mars Lumograph 3B   FBI Bottlecaps

    Timesine (Taliesin)

                        Daft Pflanze /
      Hayrick Glam

(and my favorite   title, anyway) :

TOTALLY HARROWING DR
last night. Mostly just freaked out that the right axle on the car (Mom and Dad's Subaru)
is ready to crack. Tried for Bolinas ended up in Dogtown pop. 33 hand-dabbed on the
silvered green sign in black paint 34 35 36 (and back down)—my nerves were shot ever
since MUIR BEACH where I got out to pee in the <u>dark</u> with the smash and tremble of the
ocean in my face—then back up through the fogline along the black pitching cliff-kettled
Pacific which I <u>knew</u> I could sight if I tried (but didn't wanna) down my mind in the fog.
A clapboard camper was pulled off along the road at the stage doors of Muir Woods and
I saw faces in bright kitchen porthole sawn-out in profile with wavy seagull-white hair.
WHAT LOOKS GOOD TODAY? Then up and down these fogbound tunnels and tree
evacuations with the invisible censor just out there <u>pulverizing</u> and being outside of time

as a fact. There was no hospitable place to pull off—through Olema and Pt. Reyes Stn. and over the Lagunitas bridge considering stopping but feeling too conspicuous actually torn between a desire for company (night lights, the sound of folks taking out garbage) and a secluded Sequoian awning to wake up under in the steep morn shadows of the ocean. - - - - - - - But heading inland, whimming sleepily to Nicosio and casing the place—a village with a scrappy little league diamond for a heart, Guy [Will—ed.] LaFranchi Park, and parking there to sleep at the gates of the severe starched peak of Old St. Mary's Church (1867) across the rubber f/ Druid's Hall … woke up at 5:10 a.m. after oh 5 hours sleeping rockily in the back of the car folded down in KM's old army sleeping bag. THE SKINNY ON HEROICS. No further out than San Rafael and all I really want to do after 4 cups of coffee at Lundy's is go back to sleep. Good old metallic diner onions in a heap on the nacreous skillet. Really, there's no better place to be than this diner still I gotta go—south I think. Who said always leave big tips for breakfast waitresses? The Justice System. As I was falling asleep I kept insisting on a San Quentin all made of ice.

.   .   .   .

Noel,   1.17.12

Actually I doubt much of that architecture stuff will make it into the poem, but who knows? I've been writing these poems since Tangier that circulate through CA and it finally occurred to me that I was doing it—writing poems from a spectral CA boardwalk town called Planta Nova. By reading all the architecture books and plant books now I'm trying to create solid grounded mental conditions for the poem to move through. Leave home. The poem is supposed to be a mover inside or an <u>unroller</u> of this molten West that I've habitually come to in burst-memories, hunches, but now I'm reading to ground it in actual … you know … actual plants and balcony rails and shivering SF Headlands barracks or Painted Ladies in decline. How did these things get here made by hand or sown by "seeds caught in animals' hair" when gold diggers came on boats? What's the name of all that dry cable-vine grass growing in the sand drifts on the other side of beach highways?

The Goalies of Eldritch are a "troupe" of outsiders who aren't actually aware of each other's existence. And "The Yarrows" is documentary poetry where I set out to make memory from scratch. Another reason I'm reading CA documentary stuff. But it's important that the writing isn't "narrative" from a distinct POV—I want it to be like something overheard, or like coming into a movie in the middle or someone's crackpot gossipy LECTURE … but I want the background to confirm that it's a True Story … and to rip off the ace card from linear Narrative:

                              Momentum!
                                              the just-add-water farmer
                    with his soup can prosthetic
        a butterfly early

                        warning system
                                    the eclipse splinter
    the shin guard grass blade fossil minter
                                        biked to the Ice Capades
    with the Scarecrow Vato
                        fee fie shoeshine 2-bit rhino rodeo
                                                    the
    cocoa hay late-nite
                    lost cause contralto
                                Mikado ham radio
    cream pie kamikaze

and to intersperse the rushes with snapshots of "Goalies" like the early run of the poem ...
Kyoto Showboat etc ... which also cross the nightmare fairgrounds of the CA described—
the kinda D&D geekishness of the troupe's title meant to reflect this notion of a play-
acting Guild of Freaks.

I'm completely back and forth on the value—of the <u>why</u> of the <u>what</u> I'm doing with this
poem. It seems absurd just now to write a self-consciously ambitious poem and I wonder
if it all seems jumbled and flat from the outside looking in, as it does to me today. But I
can't keep writing poems the way I was writing them over the last couple of years (or earlier
than that) and I want to jam rhythms together—dice iambs over motheaten sweaters and
vandalize the state.

In some radical and maybe foolish sense the poem is supposed to Show not Tell—as in:
If Cija Bellis (a friend) slits her wrists but doesn't die, and the poet (speaking) ends up
celebrating by buying a flower and visiting a palmist where Cija herself shows him that
her wrists have closed (as she reads his palm) before she "goes undercover" in the most
ludicrous way (as a double-agent Nazi with lipstick on her teeth) in order to tell his
future—before drifting through an Indian Summer carnival to hit the "old roads" with
her phantom troupe—well ... I want all of that to happen IN CAMERA, no cue cards
posted or Explanations ... and I realize that this means the poem may be TOTALLY
CONFUSING unless, somehow, I'm able to get the reader to follow what I hope to be
bright word shots into the dark ahead ... I feel like the language has got to be very very
high to get away with breaking so many windows ...

THE GOALIES OF ELDRITCH so far

Nice, the Interflora foil placed in the menagerie
a pole away
from the cell phone shop
and Omega of the subway cave

like a paper cup of lemon ice
            could be, when you're sick.

And a friend calls to tell you
Cija Bellis didn't die—
You buy a white carnation
and wear it to the palmist's, hard by
the ticket booth in the station.

And when she turns your hand over
you see her wrists have closed.

It seems to fit. Happy she's alive—a bit

like being sent in pieces to your past, past feeling
dumb sirens tumble on the ceiling.

She went undercover,
her Swastika arm band
turned her panties pink
            —Sang down parachutists
with lipstick on her teeth.
Made the enemy sing
and shucked his tongue
when he stuck it in her ear—
With the same air she had of not being

sure, or there
as though her skin were weather,
that I remember:

The same shying hands as her fingers spread
like electrified rivers
across the card table,
and she told your future as a fable...

The tonsured mallet
that launched the slug that sprang
the fire bell
—smooth jack that took the blow

The beer can by an instep
clipped,
the garden snail
majordomo
foreclosed by lye

Water pistols pinpointing pinwheels filling
punchy balloons
Root beer candy stick
vampire fangs
Nacho lingerie
splayed on generator grate
Waspish motorbike
chained to fence stakes...

—Crossroads waver in dark heat
Halogen fairies on sizzling meat
—One Goalie sought her shadow cast
Hole in the Bucket
closing fast

Chico   Mariposa   San Rafael

Eureka

Hole in the Bucket closing fast

Lakeport   Redding   Los
Gatos

Hat Creek

Hole in the Bucket closing fast

Fort

BRAGG

m   e   n   d   o   c   i   n   o

          Enci   no

Nevada City

Hole in the Bucket closing fast

                    Fruitvale   Pasa

dena   Dublin   ECHO PARK

      Hole in the Bucket closing fast

...Let her sleep
a little bit, just
enough to get back
her dream
           , passed out beat
on Mokelumne Hill
spit and grass blades
printing her cheek

46

Dean?
him   in the motel rm.
you?"   Shitsorm stay-
staying, storm shades drawn   way redwood   mezza-
wait
        They   live ant in toothpaste
a
New   loop
went   tumblers   loop   2
know,   fingers   (Grizzly Peak
        It   bikini top moldering
In early spring. The *conscripted greens*
so   on the wall-
Virginia   vintage
        The   cathode
stopped   able   ermine
hunting   cracked   her eyeball
road   sable   airline his
to   life story.
        . They
they   — marked by a single event: when he pulled out a semi-
automatic pistol and shot a pregnant pig at a petting zoo.
couldn't   horrible)
        Justin   . Their house always smelled like fresh-
baked cookies — some kind of undersugared Snickerdoodle
concerned.
the harp   embedded
wouldn't, all those flat gray sharp
        But   as though stuck in fizzled muscles) scat,
ragged oak leaf
beat   the grasstips, pink
matches
pushed
him
after
        It   casional hiker's clew
long,   peel shred
days
came

                        petal from curbside bouquet

*

Interviewer: With the new show, some people are saying that you've tried to do too much.

Ravelstein: I don't think they'd know too much if they saw it.

*

the Yarrows. Of course owing to the situation

row "Pile"   lost on the run

man, pillow fluff   location scout for Hitchcock's *Birds*. He

ears   dollars, a California Gothic mansion

        cherry creamsicle rosette

mocking, flicking at the frayed nylon string on the tether pole

most   Sally Yarrow.   ripped silk cushions

rusting porch screen.

        It   grouchy fatalist with transparent sentimental apparatus,

        Jed Yarrow Sr.

was night. Pine needles tipped

pissed in Pt. Reyes Station   So the "curse"

very   New

Carlotta;   Amsterdam Avenue, finding an echo of the longing he ex-

foliated in her hothouse.   thirty-five at

thick with old-growth tar   in   books for a liv-

        . Villa Montezuma

that   work, means you'll never make any money!"

Jed,

house—the paint flake off the

Castle   boot tooth mold made in the mud, perceived

the curled flake on the star-shaped thistle.   That

                        sappy. But he wanted

wanted   , esp. Carlotta's

Prieta, ripping the lanes like wet paper

Art   shattered like blown dandelions,

the chimney, drunk   "Are you nuts, or kidding?"

        Sally

her nickname) her cobweb skin flung with Sudafed moles

tether pole under the buzzing streetlamp...

                        *   *   *

                Three days after the big speech at N.O.W.   sick.
When Eloise
them   they
metastasized   Art
was   got
as   because
Art
all   any
Jed and Sally. He
while   Folgers tin of small change just inside the glass
hothouse door

m
  a
    g
      i
        c

a
 l
  a
   l
    m
     o
      n
       d
        w
         a
          w
           a
            n
             d

finds a   "K" Line   brooding in   T
                                    I
                                    L
                                    E   out +

up from the mister

                 the tile moves like skin over muscle

Where Sally sees the "adolescent
Triceratops" grazing
in loomy fern brake, feels
vertigo then realizes
the "nature" she has
chanced on is all diorama—climbing hand
over hand up the guide rail to the floodlit landing strip
of Anthropology,
Greek revival weeping tallow
straight from the Potomac—Sassafras
fairie ring daffodils and Ruffles transponders
The Bureau of American Prosody
       —ethnoprosody—
          —technoprosody—
                    "freelancing"
city hungers out to Cheyenne
via Reno
per Greyhound ($100 roundtrip
to Jefferson—worms—
               and embargo)
72 hrs in the Paleo-bionic
Meat is Murder t-shirt from a Wyo. thrift store
        —and never lost
her *Centeer*
Sunset at the western door, 9
cloves of hallowed garlic for the Wiccan OCD
dubstep—the denizens of noteryear
in the Sutro labyrinth
bless Kryptonite key, sparking sage at 4 points
quick set starry eyes in China Village
grown bolder—mussels fried in crumbs
panned out on the docks.
And the wild boat whitened the bay
of The Hectic Merrimack
     all dressed in
        black
             on that eastbound non-stick bus
where successive powers fell away
shifting her toward
"more intimate and disorienting relation"
said her fortune cookie...

"and one for the cut worm"

EAR BONES

PLANTA NOVA DEPT. OF TOURISM

Subject: "Getting There"
Attn: Brain Maciel (DEEP BACKGROUND)

Pls proof copy for intro to "Planta Nova & Environs"

VISIT PLANTA NOVA
                              Beach Boardwalk where they serve you
Bone
Ice Cream, Hair
Ice Cream   Software
hull of horse
chestnut & crack
shot flintlock
—an integral scoop whiter than white & bloodshot
Bat bras
lapping the
lungs
       AIR   CANE   LAVA   LAIR
melt-in-your-mouth
Filo Bux & Cupids
deepfried in uranium. At the CIA
Plant / Alien
          Plant the peach wallpaper burns itself
into the mind of even one-
               time customers
as does the faint
but quaffable
hunch that the sullen youth packing scoopers look
too akin to bats to be accidental—In
fact they hock loogies into
the (frostbitten) tubs when
things slow down +
raindrops spiral
in the Iron—like a carrot, a
lacy steel erector set
carrot—Tower
at the north end of the board-
walk

      And the graffiti!

Out on the breeze blocks reminiscent
of adobe
—the sea wall commencing, in effect
to melt into the beach
dunes (o'erspread by the hideous
"Master Key Suites"
like a giant dwarf Hibachi Moth
cocoon chopped in two)—Tags getting ruder
as they near
obscurity and the tide...

> *The Internet is full of Shitt*
> *Steve Obs wore purple tites*
> *Hugo Chavez is a purple baboon*

> *UR Mai CD Hombray fl*
> *Columbia hairball Mixtal*
> *Quetzylyentl*
> *like Dustbustin Hoofman*
> *on an Archipelago*

cija bellis sucks nazi dick

(her mind

a sanctuary for doomed
        thots)

The other lady across the table—I mean these are *nice people*—insists that when she was in high school in the Bronx sixty years ago the girls wore 30s-style "shirt" swimsuits—"literally"—while the boys in adjacent lap pool, separated from the girls by a thick rolling wood wall, swam *buck naked*, and one fine day the boys—. Madeline scoffs. But after all she was not raised in the Bronx but in Brooklyn.

She goes on and on about dogs and insists hers stopped eating when the groom implied he was fat. Rob won't hear it. "Dogs, dogs will eat *anything*," he says more than once. But he's not debating her, it's clear, not exactly. Just pleading an exasperating, indubitable fact about dogs. I can see he's in pain. Now the doorbell is ringing nonstop and Rob introduces me to the new guests, but this lady overhears...

Her: What was it he said you are—eh?—a poet?
Me: A poet, yeah.
Her: (Consolingly) That's *OK*. To be a poet. I think poets are *good*.
        (Utterly, blithely)—I think orange sweaters are good too.
Me: Is this sweater orange?

jellied turds found out on spits
and drops of dandy pee

"—at the Eldritch Sweet Shop."

"Old Hollywood studs on Crystal Cove in white terrycloth robes, their oiled black hair glimpsed through Chinese screens."

"'At least they don't butter their hair'—Rimbaud."

"'Cos they totally tore up Moro Beach," adds T.J., a native. Nevertheless the bloodless coup that deposed the L.A. streetcar (back when high school boys swam naked in the Bronx) is news to him. Perfectly good news.

"—a Troubadour, or a short hand, mangled on the breakrocks."

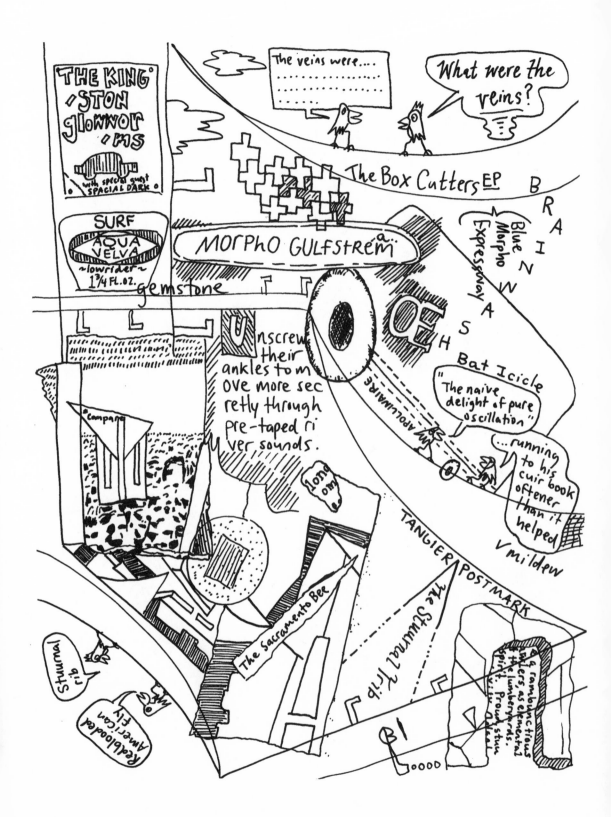

WAY TO WEST
#12

Cigars from Havana
          illicitly lush
still may give you cancer
tho
not every question has an answer

A brush with the Havana
          dodo
in an elite humidor
or sweltering in Burbank
where the Perminator
goes straight
will not keep him from looking
like the Pillsbury Rasta

Through the backlots of Paramount
through oases and tweaking fonts
          of apocalypse by meteor,
gnawing his glorified Blunt
rides the Law and his paramour

There's no leftover Windex
for polishing cockpits
above the Bay of Pigs
and all the shepherds of the MX
are bi, immortal florists

Yet Che Guevara perseveres
like Ben Gazzara
in "The Killing of a Chinese Bookie"
to outlive his death by many years,
by smoking stogies
rolled up on the inner thighs of strippers

It's better to be coming out of nowhere
than going nowhere
                              Yeah
keep it right there
On a jet plane
              —a Commodore—
high above the elk
and, not only that
                  Nothing is going to go
wrong there to where someone is going to get
hurt.
              Are we cool?
        Copacetic, Cleopatra
it's a now brainer for
me
Bring the money, Beto
let's count it in our
wife beaters, back
up, let's
count it on your twin
bed—don't make it
don't get dressed
                        for the
wedding yet—
Flew it all the way
from L.A., let's smell it
looks good
nobody ever sat on it
nobody ever even touched this money
there were no checks and
balances
looks good under the
D.F. streetlight—
                        tops off the raven
honey bear,
the sky blowing fast and low over cardiac boardwalk
rides—greased
lightning stains the shells of clouds
                  hair-clogged drain
                  sphincter
                  veiny smoke-fringed
                        jellyfish
                  Whirling Lotus
                  pulsed in
                        HEART THROB
—some percussive digital sitar loop

spilling from the head
                              shop
                              —"get me out of here!"
        ...the air hockey thimble of my
mind becoming Plant
                    rolled under a lid of crashing
                    dirt—the tunnel
                    breaching the valley
                    the knowledge
                    I was born from the womb of a vast orb spider
                    whose birth pains are stabs of purple lightning
                    —the terror that comes with it

                         Step right up, step
                                   right up
                         let your eyes grow lean
                                   and long,
                         an anxiety so
                                        thorough
                         'twas most cozy,
                                   so
                         tireless it flew

By the church stoop...
one of the stairs is badly chipped
(must've been f/ lugging in the P.A.)
                    needs *mending*
O,
      and just across the
diamond: DRUID'S HALL
gray + spotted slung-back
cows in the yellow grasss   lichen-
splotched glacial
                         obelisk an upended
oak
        ...I notice
the liver spots on the
back of my hand as I try to stuff my freak
out in the pencil sharpener, behind the
                                        dugout
green ply
paint "donated by
                    Kunst Painting"
                    (cf. Rusty Kuntz, the Tiger)
                              sunflower + twisty
lace on the trunk of the powder

blue limo swung
                        up at Rancho Nicosio,
the bridesmaid's bare
                        ankle chiming out
the wing door
in beige suede (buckskin?)
bootie
—Chauffeur smoking on the edge of night.
Tall Irish-tinged bloke also smoking, like a lyrical pugilist.
Brown paper
sparrow nests
cram the eaves and a big ripped mossy
tree: Dusty Greensleeves—brother lives
                in the Everglades but they're still
tight—w/ solitary raspberry thistle out
                                back, and cowflops on the
weeds in the whistle-by-picture
                windows, spruce goose flies
                3 rosy green apples
                racked on porch, coral
                                innards in the tattoo
parlor w/ maraschino
                        shoulder blades, a necklace
of turquoise Nerds
OK—I'm trying to ex
                plain to the 3
tough wiry white guys all covered with browning
tattoos why I think
it's good to help the little kid, Arab
                                kid ran straight into
the rusty chain pole going down to the beach
was pumping blood from
a gash in his eyebrow ... One of them
shades out the doorway of the junkshop
says "I wouldn't
                        care if they were all" — "We should
take out tanks and shovel
'em into the ground and bury them alive"
—I realize they now mean to kill me,
had only been amusing me
as I tried to ex
                plain why it was so
crucial the doctor stitch the kid up and how
none of their objections
                                mattered
the war / the "enemy" didn't

matter it was so
"irrational" and I was so
fervent—is what they hated:
That I was thrilling to my goody goody ass so very much
I
    did a crap job at enlightening them
to the basic thing—
                    Just goes to
show,
There are as many ways of fooling yourself as there are
to skin a cat.
                Why,
I'm fooling myself
now just pretending I've figured that much out.
Like at 21 I was too ignorant to know
when someone was nodding out v. OD'ing,
called the cops on that guy shooting up in the
toilets,
                hallway of Neighbor to Neighbor—
Would I still make that error?
I thought he was OD'ing because he sighed and
I heard something drop and saw his needle
on the floor in the stall. When
the cops carried him out
his faced showed neutral bliss.
God, I talked to Azad and said

                        "Remember—?"
and showed him us lying
back on the hill above dusk-setting
Berkeley and I weep as I talk
to him and tell him—ask him
to forgive me—and he
                        says, coming in close
I see his whole bemused mug, death-stoned eyes
                    "For what?"
                                "For not
seeing your son, man!"
Then my head drops,
my palms go clammy
...and it's
            clear: the cliff
at Sibley with the twisted tree
crowning it, and the rope spider
web—
        and I'm pulling in on a steaming train,

sucked in by the skullery crown,
and there's a man, a
                          being, waiting for me
there, I can see his shoulder
frame, the gaps at his arms,
there is a
            stick across his
face—   —and he's talk
                      ing to me and I'm

trying to answer
fast and Russell is singing

> *Pai, afasta de mim esse cálice*
> *Pai, afasta de mim esse cálice*
> *Pai, afasta de mim esse cálice*
> *De vinho tinto de sangue*

and it's beautiful, I
                    want to sing now, I think
"Can we sing?" and
move my mouth as he
sings...
            and then I'm <u>out</u>   in the heat waves
the phone numbers
painted on the side of the tow truck
waver
            and turn into Hebrew lettering.
The witch turns her head to look at me
(she's wearing neon green sneakers
                plasticized silver logo
                matches the sprinkler system on the dark
morning traffic island)
Witches.
It's hard to believe this one retains a human core, her
face is so grooved and twisted—That's
bullshit, man
she's an adept
            surefire eyes
                        she must've slowed down
her heart
forest all around
                    comes into sync.
But I <u>didn't</u> know the witches were training
                        young girls...
The slope with all the
poison oak and the

twisted oaks and wet
dashed leaves starts
screaming then lifts
its wings its claws still buried
in dead stripped bark and
things and opens its fruitcake bat
mouth and scre
                    ams. This is the
power of the witches, to scare away the lilylivered
                    naysayers—
The black smoke is supposed to look like its blasting
from the bat's mouth but it's so obviously been
patched in in the film lab.
I want to spend the morning in that lab, toasty warm,
not stuck on the edge of the witches' garden
so conventionally well-tended,
rows of common innocuous flowers
                              (name them!)
Shouldn't really come as a surprise.
But how wrong you were
about witches, as your own
                         daughter could've told you
if you'd know enough to ask!
Get back to the car and try to sleep but
can't—someone's already
sleeping there. Russell
is gone
but another homeless guy, who looks a whole lot
like him
is there.
Russell, I know it's not you, it's not some *Lady
Vanishes* scenario
though you're a great film head.
I know I gave you a real-life

                    newspaper:

THE PLANTA NOVA NOW

    Now you wouldn't have
seen it happening
in Winters. No one here's
a racist, I
mean—N. and the Bengston
twins and I were all set to go
        rain on their parade when
Alice—and
if you believe this you'll believe—
you know
the rest. But
you oughta this time
'cos it's true: believe anything.
The White Aryan Nation

was marching past the cafe on Main when
Charlie Bengston's wife—He calls me, "There's
water all over the stair—" The whole way
up to the hospital I'm thinking
This
should be—I mean, This should be
        happening in a <u>hot</u> <u>rod</u>,
        the 2 white
            doors fly open and I
come out
of Alice's cunt
and I'm lying there scre
           aming, covered in blood.
Pure claymation terror
where they have to move my detached clay
eyelids down bit
        by bit to blink, highly

laborious, while in real
life it happened
all in an instant.
The color of wet clay
I look terrified, my
face looks like it's made outta clay, my
                <u>eyeballs</u> look like white
clay shifting in terror from Alice
to Charlie, Alice
smoking, propped up in bed and
Charlie staring into my face like a little
boy—

          —

                —

Don't want to creep anyone out just sitting here
so turn the key—up past the red Chinese screen
Gothic Steak House
Plush Jennifer Convertible
showroom
little windows in the sky,
nice balconies
smell of grilled steak
eggplant
little people taking the
plane
    —a Commodore—
sweet kernel heads white
+ yellow, you don't even
have to steam

                  (opens her eyes)

"Lentils of invention
          chase Reagan's jelly beans
thru Saturn's rings
to the Garden of Fads.

                frothy
                    airy
                        square

        Fission
        'leftover' from
                the primorbial fire
ball that befell

Nothingy

—Era of the Sun-
          beam Lamb
Chipper,
               the Alzheimer's
                    Assn pencil
     unsharpened
     in reusable ceramic
                    yogurt cup—
     multifaceted
     pink bead
               on the kitchen sill.

     Raw American ache
               threading out on phantom
               ganglia of Ike's
               bitumen octo
               pus

                    —Generation-skipping hipster abolitionists
hitchhike through the dust bowl
               glyphed in a speck of Monsanto corn
just as Nerds
          glyph root canals
                    in Crips blue.

Praise God
who is everything, the one and only, indivisible
all at once
          all frailty, all failure, all fuck.
Star Trek
          the series,
Star Trek
          the coffee mug—"

                    (she laughs)

"in the '79 Insula all splattered with gnats."

.   .   .   .

But that's not even true even true.
Sally came from up past Pt
Reyes Stn, echt
Gualala, it's a whole other Sally
I'm on about, local lore

Lady though she may one day
be, this is way back when
Tosh
Dizney (sic) stuck a stick in her
lazy
eye, and it ran straight out like
a hat rack on Eye Hill, Mom
Eloise gunning the pink
Insula off flood mats to the ER in
uh
Knot Sure Whare
Ordered Sally
Sit on both hands and sing, the back-
seat bench left tingling
pie charts on the red backs
of her hands. That damn Dizney kid
was a ton of bubbles, I tell yuh, his dad was
a rich dick, some kind of
brain doctor who owned
Regret's foal Nemesis, placed at
Preakness and was the one who
actually sold Dilan Hole in the
Bucket.
Key bit of backstory, that.
Tosh Dizney got his mom's
cheekbones and Sally put up with
him which for her was like going
steady but I never did get it, he
was a spoilt ruther sullen kid tho
beau and fairly toned by ice
money. Golden baby shoes
on the bottom of the bottomless lake
of money. A Lago di Lettuce,
Poor Franklin in the Lake, drowned
"Stonewall" eats mirror
short ribs in carnations spelling
Chloride City, Brendan
"Zazu" Dizney first came in the Silver
Rush made a mint selling picks to
the daft, hydraulic furniture,

bought half of Planta Nova by the
sea in fact the Tiger whirlmagee
purrs on coals now of the first
Dizney manor gone up in flames
as the Strange Attractor
dived, rattling like a string of coal cars
coming down
a hand-turned dune.
Bone cancer. Totally. Total
coincidence about Eloise. Hers. I
think she and
what the hell was his name? I mean that's why it
may seem more than
a coincidence (but nothing is) since
they were having an affair it was rumored.
Do you buy it? You
could see it in Dilan's face
his sister getting fucked by that prick, supposedly.
Ha ha, I don't see it. No.
But there was plenty of chin music.
I think people resent class because they
don't see where it comes from, a
classy person is like a mystery
book missing pages. They can be
poor but it's easier to be from old money that ran thin,
that kind of honorary pathos—

                    Mighty Oak
          Intaglio
                              Better Luck Next Time
          Fortune Cookie
                              Dark Wand

—Sally wanted to see them trot out
Of their splintery fairy chests
Scummy hoofs toasted over shelled hearts
She thought there should be gold banners like
butter, Homage to Elephant. Hole
in the Bucket dunked in the
rushes—one look and Sally knew
he couldn't.
She always was a good ten lives ahead
of Dilan in matters that mattered, to him
more than her: she admired

doomed Amber. It's hard to have
a perceptive kid around when
you're a gambler.
Dying from the friendly fire
of your own ironic patter. Such a
lover and so losable—I wouldn't
accuse him of being a sore loser
for instance. Dashing swinger. But
once he lost his looks, built his
handsome face matchstick by
matchstick by matchstick.
In a beer bottle—

Housepainter days at the Yarrow
Pile—arrest his decline, parted
fingers against
blue slashes, Singing—
"I shot an arrow
into the book, wither did
        it strike no letter / I rode a horse
into the cheese, verily
        it brushed no aatom."
Imagine a quiver swagged in blue
drip bucket, fanned out spaghetti
western, tipdown—

                    Twirling Candy
Gladding goes
            wire to wire   Indian Charlie Gone

West, Coolmore Dame
                    Pair of
                    Aces   OCD

Mile stamina Light stakes by Macho see more Wild Astrology Soldat Gulfstream Queen

Suave Chapel, Roar of Black
Wonders, Hear no Mumbo, Indian
Gold, Cutlass Fax

Wold wir. Wildcat Media. Dwindle Whipper. Strong Wink. Halo's Mandate.

Puerto Rico Napkin. Charlie Thyme. Cool Coal Midge.

slap you with a lawsuit. $ome Sinophobic flanneur simmering in the poke.

Enamored with Florentine enamel, Hugh Manatee CAN be
saved. Transcendental Papoose. You send me!

     Epilogue: Paul Molitor rode a Gila Monster to the East River.
     Then he commissioned a Gila Monster mosaic from Ted Burner's sister.

Jag, Sam went up to the chocolate carwash.
What's up with that? It's in Spreightstown but it's not locally owned.

Sally was the grand
dame of Spreightstown and
shegrew moon squashes, she
had a butte garden with eastern
exposure and her little redwood
shack was at

the foot, her screen deck she-
herself-built in a "spray" of
fuscias or dahlias, white dahlias
and little white phone booths
and Sally "It's not short

for anything!" had toughed out
the scabs in '38 the corruption
of Liebe, of Woman's Lib, Ghost
Strub the Train Tie Bull and other
Mendicants

.   .   .   .

Hare-brained conclusion, hare-brained
And ass-eared, copacetic
Dragonfly pinioned in twitching wisps
On burro Mandarin
To find her brother in Manhattan
And lure him from some sprecken ze ticklish tryst
With a journeyman actress
The story went—but as much to see Jagadis
(They'd only just met
At the bonfire on Ocean Beach), Sally

/

sassafrasses and other deciduous trees must
sprout and grow from seeds of their own kind"

Hesse!
Sally loves you

Owling
cloves in the grooved pipe
like a huge cement toilet paper tube
with Roberto Clemente
intensity, George Van
Gogh threw a Led Zep whip cream one-hitter
at Jed's head—
Jimi!

* be cheerful

on Gr undhog Day
* or lucky

still loaded
with smoking Paisley Cohosh. Rambled with the Van Goghs, Crazy 8's
to Marine World

Africa USA one Indian Summer
day, Jed, Sally,
George,
Mr. Van Gogh astride Hot Rats in the rose window
of the clapped-out Chinook
sunroof cracked
. Waterslide

Wet handprints on redwood rails

"flat" girls in bikinis

Bloodwarm water rushing green fiberglass boulders

George, 14, crushed out on Sally
12
     the noon in his eyes

And how the shushing water carried her away
like a laughing can opener, shorts bunched at the thighs

Banana taffy for the ride

*

Concurrently

"That night," said Ravelstein, "I was riding up the dark marsh
road, cop cars race past with more and more frequency, running off
the dark like silver prints

         'til I'm running in a bottleneck of sirens, shift
down along the cliffs—same bend where your dad totaled

the pink Insula, 'pinballed into a sand bank on Bolinas
Lagoon'
     (Marin Independent)
         and walked away ... Marsh dredged
at dawn,
an affront to the plovers,
five fishermen buttonholed to wring their caps
and the wreck interred
at Florian's Yunkjard
inland.
     Its giblets hooked and liver pickled:
Florian's horse lips in the car's mouth
mirror like a 2-way spyglass

     —he pops it free with the amber flat screwdriver—

Boxing gloves necking white-gold on a big nail
in the dead car barn.
Where he keeps the triplicate credit slips and gummed receipt pads
in complaining gray metal desk.
     Hey,
       ask Florian who belongs to those gloves!

—'til I see they're floating up,
the sirens, across the shoulder just around the bend where Art
bought it, and shift down, wondering

'speed trap?'
'dragnet?'

'fire drill?'

: It's
as I'm crawling by I see all the types, the
Indian Summer Stock—
squalling kids. big-ankle moms. mid-
dleage men in checked shorts.
jack-knifed lawn chairs.
motor homes.
dozens of them.
a caravan
packed into the cliffs, the sulfuric floodlit cliffs
washed by the silent tumble of sirens..."

(Sally scrolls down,

furnishing line breaks

between sips of cold tea   like watered whisky

in the Asperger Heaven of Art's study)

"Cija Bellis is ... what?

According to an old friend I just bumped into, Brain Maciel
—is now a medium or fortune teller of some kind. It seems to fit.
And has a 'psychosexual condition,' this according to herself,
where she can only get to know a person by feeling them up."

Crushed cans of humanity with the meat sucked out
Poached ghosts smashed with forks
Automatic sacrifice
Atomic novellas
Forests milled in OPEC rainbows
Isuzus
Sunbeams
At least one other '79 Insula
—shrimp, not pink—
went down the Peninsula

                on a Big Gulp Wrecker
        flatbed truck
                        w/ a yarn-trimmed
                            Virgin of Guadalupe
spinning in the cab

CANDLERS
ice cream & soda fountain   w/ its   .
white + blue neon
chip off the old
iceberg   on the counter

rubber ring red + gold neon:

                    Occidental East
                    Brewers

Young Mexican crew

hangs back—they fill Sally's cup:

MY

F
R
I
E
N
D
,
H
E
N
R
Y

M
I
L
L
E
R

U
tah
"cross
roads of
the We
st"

~1897~   ~1787~

N
ew
Jers
ey "cr
ossroads
of the
Rev
ol
ut
i
o
n
"

\
M
a
r
s
L
u
m
o
g
r
a
p
h
3
B

The letter in front of her, pace her soft pack:

STASI NUMEN

"your fear is blocked perception of a vast awakening"
—Tony Norris, e-mail <u>non</u> <u>local</u> <u>waves</u>

Hi Jed, I'd say American
                              democracy was fifty years behind abstract expression-
ism
when Occupy broke
                    crossing civil
                                        insurrection and
homelessness
              in America
is not supposed to be
political
                         He or she lives
                                          in a finished state. of police.
Politicians don't identify   They have no identity

in the daily procedure.   I'm living in another America
                           They call me an elective beggar
When—if
              I fall asleep my civil rights
are illegal
                    The mayor reads my silence as a sailor's wave.

In their latent state civil
                        rights "may exist for an indefinite time"

              "reliques of sensation" —Coleridge. The political

class in America possesses a film strip made of bold abstractions
to project shades of rhetoric
                              onto all available media
Dizzy
to categorize and evaluate an emergency
like Occupy

"We hold these truths self-evident"
                      that the blood under the microscope has been tainted or even
swiped

by an insurgent
   mother
        tongue.

        Homeless society has its own currency, its laurel
           leaf.

dirty politics?—now what other?

          *

          Jed,

Poetry is language

And the poet who does the work liberates the language.

What is "experiment" to that? Yet you can't stop rocking

the plastic brass
            Blasts from the Photon Suit. Memory sensibility

your ethics. Conscious bells of justice

tap into deeper waters you can't touch
dreams, blocked
          Mostly a mystery
plus

lots of other people, too. Far from an event

Experience is a process—Just thinking about
it there is a,
      uh
        artifact of breaking events being translated

lugged into this very wild pursuit

called out
by some evolutionary finger,

Zuccotti Park on Halloween

        and flashes going off like someone snapped

a velvet sheet of diamonds in the air.

A woman tourist in red cashmere blazer gazing up

the sidewalks spilled

into the bus lane

McDonalds press box. A glass elevator

.   .   .   .

"soft hums iced"
—Brian Lucas

C.B.B.
      estranged from his hum-
anity
    by poisons his
           shoulder crushed when he rubbed his eyes
his chakras
        nibbled by rats—hung batlike in the jacket of an Apache
GI
    to transact survival, his lamb at heel trembling
and invisible to most
           as the rubble that ulcerates
his skull is invisible
so that their ankles cut through it like roots
                where he botches
the most basic conjugation
in the dream of the language they lay open

—Coins
      drop into his souvenir plastic cup
a clam
    of tempeh on the edge
            of the corner trashcan's wedding
      tent (which melted
          runs to snot) makes it to his blanket
rolled out on the sidewalk
        next to his sleeping dog, Clay:

Quite well
I'm glad to say—it's a warm night in San Rafael
with a harvest moon
       over the Innerstate
       and a red red wedge of watermelon
drips in his fingers
: the seeds are nice to spit—"Hey
        thanks!" he calls after
Sally, "what's your name?"
as she cuts across
      the watermelon-veined marquee
of the CA Film Institute:

      Animated Shorts

        ...ditching

the reveling picnickers
then on all fours
        mangling the slope of gray
                snouts—gray snouts—
of some edible sea
lion that dies en masse
whose snouts compact and smear like damp gray
dunes as she harvests them
with the small cutting
board, singing a song
to their spirits

      Paper Sausage Gun
      It's such a good lion
      O it's still a-groin

all the way out to the train tracks drumming refineries
(The Iron Triangle)
slicing 'cross tracts fickly slapped up even for slums
blowing with cracked plastic things
like a tide went out
and kept going out

      Paper Sausage Gun
      It's such a good lion
      O it's still a-groin

to rapidly gentrifying blighted rowhouses in w/
coiling gates on all varieties of body
shop, this one now
some performance art space
+ robot junkyard
crammed with the ruins of grueling wandering
carnivals, a kind of accordion car
with pedals, ringmaster's pulpit handrails
splintered like fire crackers
and there—unmistakably—the BANDSTAND
from the Yarrow wedding, just an edge
visible: the cornflower bunting
once gay as bachelor's crepe, as faked by Eloise in white
and blue house paint blended
with a pastry basting brush

Weathering a myld catatonia
For the windfall speculators of bohemia.

.　　　.　　　.　　　.　　　.　　　.　　　.

The day before the day before
The eight-alarm fire
                     at
                              S. Heterogeneity and Penrose
Ave.
Razed the Democratic Party
Beer hall to the dregs, Jed Yarrow made
A fist on the porch of the prior
                              mission—But it was more like knocking

A giant book for luck and getting
                           leaden choirs.
From the genie soy in Iowa to the Beltway Sniper
It boded badly, he decided, for the party of Mondale/Maserato.
While the hard water smells of Antonio's Prell
Came off his scalp in aseptic Central
Valley morning sun: It was going to be a hot one. Admitted

By the young aide, a copious dose of brilliantine
Unable to tame his rock 'n' roll hair, and peeling off
The Strange Attractor 50th Anniversary
Windbreaker with a snap of static Jed instantly (his heart
Grew gills) pegged his tribal peer for the day as
None other than the lead singer of the very band to have opened the triple bill

Hours earlier at The Open Door:
Who'd strummed a custard Stratocaster
Shapelier than himself, black lock
Licking down,
Doll hand with thumb of elf
Festooning slant pick ups,
Barring the neck—In pegged pants and Cuban boots
He stood 5 foot 2
Or so, Jed would guess
When passing him out the door of the toilets swollen with turds

And swollen toilet paper, his ears still ringing with the too
Strident changes they'd rung on New Wave ladders
—Though they had one song that made nothing else matter.

Don't you understand? I didn't want to get roped in to your crazy back and forth. That's why I didn't write, sounded distant on the phone because I was distant. I'm 3000 miles away! Can't

*you see that I just wasn't <u>interested</u> in getting with your neurotic, narcissistic melodramatic
potlatch of love notes and phone calls late into the night full of pretentious small talk. Fuck
that noise. I'm in love with you!*

Jed: "If a total stranger I didn't know really well
Were to come in wearing a beanie, a soul patch,
A bolo tie with a turquoise catch,
Two-tone mohair creepers, a dashiki,
Vuarnet sunglasses on a dayglo neck string,
His freckles like flecks of cocoa in milk,
Spit-crusted
Cheek lined by the throw pillow
Ramp to the bay window onto swing set and Sky
Mall birdbath in the back yard where N. and his wife now pass
Evenings and the megalomania leaves turning
Brown snap cleanly—Were to come
In, this caption dreamer, while Delta Blues carve up the moon's
Sax lesson
Like lean blue canvases
And whirlpools in raw steak
Pressed to a smokestack shiner by fingers gushing
Elimination of the *exuberantly distractible*
Beloved, A Mirror Car (or, A Mirror KKKar)
Straight into the Styx
Fans muting the Oakland Coliseum parking lot splashed with burning sulfur
Kliegs and lashings of Dutch Master walrus mustaches, cut-off
Jeans, Thai Stick, American
                                        blues, jazz, cartoons,
            American poetry, poets,
                                    blues singers, punk rock,
                matzo ball soup on the Lower East Side, huge
                        public parks and transatlantic steamers
                redwood saunas
                                and boa constrictor iron-ons
—And were to finish his song
And pass me at the bathroom, whose floor is tile
Like grouted Chiclets, all glitter stripped
To the handsome wax of the lead singer who was offhand
And returned to his people
To pee, get a beer, and watch the next band—"

/

"Long distance food from nowhere," Jed told the chip.
"The Loneliness of the Long Distance Food from Nowhere"—Antonio.
Jed,
wiping the archetypical
                              aunt's lipstick off his cheek:
"The Boniness of the Long Distance Dude from Flaubert."
"Flaubert and Ernie"
                        sd Antonio.

green neon
                "the

last thing he saw" the

...the smell of crushed rose petals

            Petain roses

The smell of carnations at gunpoint

The smell of fresh-whacked grass

        "Someone walked off with my exacto blade—"
        And now you can't dig the moss out of your belt buckle. Donderdag.
        People are making love
                                in the suburbs, plum blossom
on the ping pong table
            like the half-popped kernel
                                of a ping pong ball
                                    —the raccoon

(*Procyon lotor*) perched
there like a bowling ball
                        chalked by a Tootsie
Roll in their rearview
                    weivraer :
The drained aquarium they'd come to drink in,
a wide grotto hall, west
wing of the Anthro bldg
Midnight or double
Frosted pot holes on lab doors double
the shadow of his solar-powered beanie...

Whose?
(the coke-black wrench in his hand withdrawn)
            St. Jello's

said Antonio,

        St. Jello of the Camper Van. Presently fumigating the epidermal ruminants of the Western Jungle with a dinged-up tea ball not even Hi-Chew wanted. There he is. Check out that glitter iron-on heart

of stone! (Tips up the bottle.) This beer is going to take the good and steady edge right off the figment field—

. . . .

UNDER THE CEMENT MOON

. . . .

she went through
w/ it:
married a barber
who eats hair

Secret kink! To which Cija,
startled
beneath the mystic's veneer
responds,
"Your chart is on fire
It's time to replace
yr old frying pans"

CLICKING HER ELECTRONIC CIGARETTE

in the Lite-Brite arroyo,
her coyote mint fan
rippling granite static
on vast Sierran screens

THROUGH PROLIX (pop.
cherry cherry cherry) to Austere,
CA
—frogs and fawns
on the golf links
at daybreak, searchlights hit
THE SUSPECT
bounding color
wheel landings
"in a headdress of what appears to be
Arabic typewriter keys—"

"Three radio patrol cars rolled up on the museum's entrance"
—The officer in training

recalls little but that the exhibit was called BLACK BART STOPS HERE
and that a Danish painter by the name of Knut Merrild (1894-1954)
was doing drip, what he termed "flux"
painting, years before Pollock;
a few stray words
"burning flowers they like to sit near"—in connection to names:

Terry Fox, Eleanor Antin
                    "living at the western edge of the U.S."

"artists could do anything they want"

                    —Vagrant Meridian—

        where palm trees crop up like blackout sky rockets

"While the debris was still smoldering

            we ventured into the rubble
            like other junkers of the community
            digging and searching but unlike others
            obsessed without quite knowing why—"

Turn that shit up said Antonio.
That's Noah Purifoy after the Watts riots.
Local artist—have you heard about this?
Went out gathering lead
drippings from melted neons—Peacock Coal
Bureaucratic Inertia
Expressive States of Doubt.
You've heard about this said Antonio.
No said Jed.
It's a long way

sd Antonio, from Black Bart shot dead
on the steps of the L.A. Museum of Contemporary Art to Black Bart shrieking
"Aw c'mon baby just give me one little taste!"
—like a Hollywood junky doing multiple takes.

BLACK BART'S OPIUM DREAM

Black Bart who will cut your throat for a nickel
Length of lace, or Black
Bart with his cardboard suitcase, increased
His creamy suit
"The color of monkey's milk"
He informs the prostitute,
With his mustache waxed, an emerald stickpin
In his cravat—
Powerwalking to Chinatown where he intends
To smoke opium for three days on end.

The hourglass of fog which is the bay
Now specked by burning ashcans on the wharfs,
Now by wicks above the wharfs sustained by gold
Ran out at noon where Black Bart crouched
On Gunshot Point,
Mocking Poins in Jeckle's voice,
His pistol like a periscope in blossoms traced
The old sawmill on Muscovite Bend
Where Primo Madrone lay in wait
In watermelon slices (one for every minute
The stage ran late) to sugar its spooking horses
When the ball from Bart's blunderbuss
Smashed out the Finnish coachman's cheek—
He swings with rein zipped round his wrist—
Engaged daughter of the Guerneville pharmacist,
Thighs bloody in the ditch—
                            ...Bart even pinched
Her dainty shoes
To flip his haircut and shave—
"Wild oats grow rank where grain once waved"

           A caricature
                    murdered by a caricature
                for a caricature of gold
             in a bad excuse for a newspaper
                   edited by a caricature
                            of an editor
                  the caricature of a drunk
              drinking the caricature of a drink
             fucking a caricatured whore

                          paying a caricatured madam
                              in caricatured haste
                  Sighting of a well-dressed man
                      with Blarneystone hands
                  paying a Chinaman with bad teeth
                          and gravy eyelids
                          in paper gold
                  the equivalent of 17, mid-aughts American
                          caricatures of gold
                  "So I feel like an extra in heaven"
                              The Tsunami Ghost Ship Meet & Greet
                      slated for low tide
                      and everyone's invited
                          —everyone and their mother

*and "otherwise why would we have come down from the sky?!" Also said, with those
shiny black bangs hanging in his pale face and little China hand on neck of Fender, "It's
the changing of the guard in the animal kingdom" to herald the moonrise. And he's
right—the 13th of Friday is a day for fucking and dancing. The witches, who need to be
(for our sake) rescued from their pointy hats + green makeup or burnt-at-the-stake
victimhood or Shakespeare Macbeth nasty wooden spoonness, were right on. <u>Mt. Diablo</u>
was where the Miwok Indians said Coyote taught God-ess how to make humans (the
Miwok selfsame) by planting feathers from 3 birds ... Condor, Crow and (I think) Hawk
in the <u>mineral dust</u> and <u>effluvium</u> and upthrust seabed peaks—projecting Xir voice from
what Whites later called the "Devil's Pulpit" ... the*

                                          Witches the
                                                  Indians the
                                                          Skaters the

Mexican day laborers

                          STOLEN HISTORY

going way back ("the One
story")—*What*
                is the motivation behind the Judeo-Christian blockbuster agent orange app?

Mt. Diablo

Heliport   Radio Tower

Buckbrush   (trunk
                          of sutured vines)

    +

Wild Lilac   ("you can smell
                          on a hot day"—Sally)

mineral
monorail, winds
driven by the rising of sun-heated air:

            No Fixed Address

Lambik
in lamb-tube voice, pitches light   rail linking carport to bio-
tech skunk
works.   Cosmic Regionalist,
                          strawberry crowns
hover from her fingertips
—a 2nd
            spectral conveyance: the mosquito
                          picked up by her hearing aid

                          takes Jed
back to Jed
Sr. / poring over
                fruitfully worthless tomes
in back of
"In Back of the Real" (gold font on L.'s
                          shop) deep
in
  to the 3rd volume of
                The Magical Ass—namely
the Parable of the Road Apple
(occasionally joined by a basking grub)
which he, Jed, crackd
at the house in Berkeley
like the one in Boumalne:
You'd step up and buy bus tickets to the Sahara, 2
tortoise shell stairs
shelved on mortared retaining wall
where traffic stops & starts—

"An exposition on the corpse of American democracy"
which died young and theoretical
which
       crackd, actually
—While popping his herpes blister by hitting on it
w/ a carpet needle
blackened over a match:
7:18 a.m. in some depilated Slurpee version of High Noon San

Antonio and all the roadies stranded outside Truckee
with dead gadgets. Sucked up in the flammable brown + bitty
blanket once wrapping the rumble seat in Jed's grandma's
camper van. Striped switch/blade/shade
by the already done
sun
and sweating while his whiskers grew
the white ace
struck off the white stucco
wall of the Seabreeze unbroken by windows—

        "Eerie hot,
         not the sun I grew up with"

—We lay down in it
where the roots of a spreading tree
capsized the grass
and K. took off her dress
and was napping naked in the fetal position
when 2 flying snails
"Matador Snails"
             hovered past *mating*
at eye level, and I shook her awake
just in time to watch them
           beep over the rose bush—
                   and K. stood up and stre
tched naked on the grass in plain view of the x'd out
windows in the bungalows just blocks
from Bullet.
And it was fine.
But I did suggest maybe she shld put back on her shirt.
And I could trick out the bra lines under her breasts.

You've never seen the Planta Nova Boardwalk so dead.
Rumors that the San Clemente nuclear plant
etc. etc.
Not even the breeze came to a head.

                    In that corner wedge
store with its display of Patti Smith chopstick
eyewear (with many doors
and all doors open wide)
and choirs of perfume vials under glass
fanciful as Mexican sugar skulls,
                              they were scooping out melty
gelato free
from crushed white tubs under lead neon piping.
K. got coffee and cheese.
I couldn't decide.
We were so carefree
you know? how a black-out can do that?
And then we were cutting through the Community

Theater, Planta Nova High—
It's become the most lavish red velveteen
thespian temple for the occasion
of early dress rehearsals for THE PIRATES OF PENZANCE, undertaken
with great expectations.
Valkyries in skin suits flutter by,
the raffish witty leads
parlay in the nosebleed seats.
I now realize that this musical is one of the greatest works of *entertainment*
—and remember every brick in town
and parachute in the jungle
of the multiplex—
The Nova Globe
at the heart of the park: Sliding doors,
mood ring lobby.
Sheer stairwells hatching further doors.
The sunken stage funky with root mold and whispering
worms inflecting cues. The light
+ sound nerve centers
notorious fire traps,
soundproofing like mud in little league cleats
                    (graffiti of the Minotaur
behind the girls' dress rack). Contrast this

to those class fittings you find in hospitals:
Red plastic plug plate,
matching cable.
Spun swabs like conductors' batons in a jar:
Special things you find only in hospitals.
Demented little objects,
sweets in a bakery

window like dusted
cutglass doorknobs. The
glazed tarts and crusts and pincushion
wish fulfillment of 70s sitcom koans on a
sugar rush—

SONGS FROM THE WESTERN JUNGLE

CARROLTON JAIL INCIDENT

Something's going on at Carrolton Jail
So many witnesses among them a hard-boiled snail

One night she she fell asleep
At the cemetery, people of all ages
Turning garlic blooms inside of her womb
When she saw herself painting with her eyelashes aflame

She was overjoyed
Then began
To chat with a reindeer
Named
Panama Sam
And became happy
Beside the tomb

O something's
Going down
At Carrolton Jail

I'll tell you how to get there
I need to get somewhere first

Realistic officers, this is the way your world looks
To us

Among the ghosts
One testified
That a bluish light
Filled the body
Of a New Orleans taxi cab driver

And a man bought a newspaper in the dark

Reptiles!

SEQUIN

Sequin played on the ro...de...o   It was

e-lec-tion day down in   Bor...ne...o   And that's why

Sequin had to play   he was a Vo-ting

Man-ta ra-a-a-ay

Sequin played on the rodeo
It was Election Day in Borneo
And that's why Sequin had to play
He was a voting manta ray

Sequin went on the ferris wheel
Fairy lights and Bethlehem Steel
It's gonna be a whole New Deal
When Sequin takes a spin on that wheel

Sequin took a ride on the Nile
He snuck under the turnstyle
The Egyptian Spring went out to see him
He was a manta ray in the museum

Sequin went to the voting poll
Struck his vote in peacock coal
Then he went flipping through the public school hall
Took his manta ray girl to the mall

Sequin went out to Oscar Grant Plaza
Took his manta ray banners to Gaza
Flew through the haunted house of Galilee
Saw the sun set on Marlboro Country

Sequin Rode on the Hobo Rails
Sent his vote in the U.S. Mail
Candy Apple ERA
Black Panther Manta Ray

Sequin played on the rodeo
It was Election Day in Borneo
And that's why Sequin had to play
He was a voting manta ray

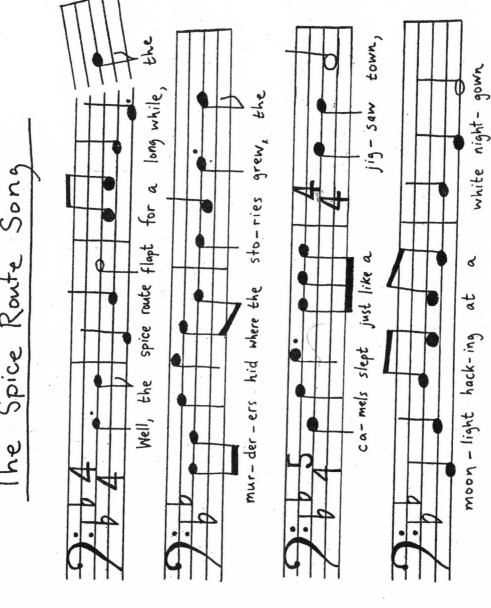

Well the spice route flapped
For a long while
The murderers hid
Where the stories grew
The camels slept
Just like a jigsaw town
Moonlight hacking
At a white nightgown

Roll 6 black marbles on a Chinese board
Throw suicide kings with bended ears
And hang bandoliers like gazelles on horns
Storm's folding in and mutiny's warm

They're searching for the nail
Of a dragon-slaying sea
Crossing up dogdays
Like a superstitious flea
Holding out for torches
On the frozen trail
Cutting up faces
To patch their sails

Peking arrows round the lip of a beer
They say the damsels smoke like bloody spears
In with the garden sparks, busdriver-tall
Famine plucks your ribcage at an impassable wall

Beards growing backward
Like a glass of stout
Shuffling satin
At the halfmoon court
The meadow cranes out
In the junkyard dawn
Kings shooting pinball
With the heads of pawns

Roll 6 black marbles on a Chinese board
Throw suicide kings with bended ears
And hang bandoliers like gazelles on horns
Storm's folding in and mutiny's warm

Love Lives of the Florida Keys

Love lives of the Flo-ri-da Keys__

East-ern Dia—mond-back just like me

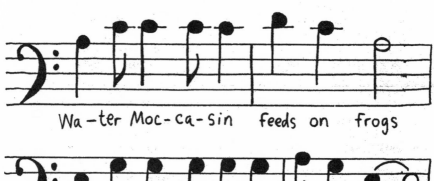

Wa—ter Moc-ca-sin feeds on frogs

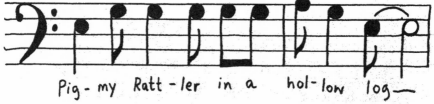

Pig-my Ratt-ler in a hol-low log__

Love lives of the Florida Keys
Eastern Diamondback just like me

Water Moccasin feeds on frog
Pigmy Rattler in a hollow log

Love lives of the Florida Keys
Eastern Diamondback just like me

Coachwhip snake, what did the bandits take?
Coral Snake in the wedding cake

Love lives of the Florida Keys
Eastern Diamondback dressed like me

Green grasshopper, 6 beating hearts
Zebra Moth in Everglades Park

Whiptail Lizard, don't look twice
Twisting on the fork of a Swallowtail Kite

Love lives of the Florida Keys
Eastern Diamondback just like me

CHEAT SHEET: Sometimes a Great Notion... Shaw on Shakespeare ... Henry IV... Henry V... The Secret Lives of Plants... Assembling CA... From Hand Ax to Laser... Mamet interviews... The Triggering Town... Eliot's essays... Untemeyer anthology... The Empire's Old Clothes... Remain to Be Seen... Prick Up Your Ears... Murakami short stories... Muthologos... Filip's book [If you Don't Go Crazy...]... Olson poems ... Cymbeline... Book on CA architecture [forgot name]... Chicago: City on the Make... Plants of the S.F. Bay Region... Conversations with Nelson Algren... Peter Pan in Kennsington Gardens... Chance Meetings... Revenge of the Lawn... Paterson... Zen Monster... Houses of Gold... Blk. Mtn. Review V.2 No.5... The Days of '49 [VANGUARD LP]... We Can't Go Home Again [FILM]... Io Earth Geography Booklet No.2... Meltzer's "6"... The Matrix of Man ... Collected Books of Jack Spicer... Bad Land [R. Emil Braun]... Nerves... Splendide Hôtel... Tabu [Brian Lucas]... Blueprint for Realist Cinema [Tom Comitta]... A Thousand Plateaus... Traffic [K. Goldsmith]... B. Andrews, C. Bernstein, various L=A=N=G=U=A=G=E + Conceptual texts online... Aevum (D2 Brazil)... Billboard Art... Dali bio... Shells in Color... The Life + Works of H. Bosch... West of the Rocky Mtns... A Dangerous Place... 20 Prose Poems [Baudelaire]... Circles Matter... Repetitions... Alpha Donut [Matvei]... Pacific Standard Time... "Trees" Golden Guide... Jane Freilicher paintings... Birds Beasts & Flowers... The Nature of the Universe ... The Trickster Shift... Cometbus #51... Notes from Irrelevance... News of a Useless Thing... Good Manners... Mercury... Mum Halo... Rd of 1000 Wonders [JjN]... The Late Show... A Feb. Sheaf... Zeroville... Rilke... The 20s [E. white]... Give Some Word... City of Pain... The Way to the Uncle Sam Hotel ... A Culture of One... Last of the ~~Mocassins~~ Moccasins

California Fairy Tales... CA Atlas [Rockwell Deluxe]... Incredible Voyage...

...Kali Yuga... Sun's Skeleton m99... Lew Welch letters [I REMAIN]...

Way Too West was printed
in an edition of five hundred copies
by McNaughton and Gunn
in Saline, Michigan in May, 2015.